La COLLECTION
by AUTOMOBILIA

CW01661465

Publisher:
Bruno Alfieri
Technical consultant:
Walter Beltrami
Editors:
Ippolito Alfieri, Silvia Giacobone
Photos:
Roberto Carrer, Gabriela Noris, Guy Mangiamele
Graphic design:
Giordano Barazzetti
Production:
Massimo Fabbri, Attilio Chiozza
Translation:
Warren McManus

INDEX

ISBN 88-85880-49-5 CL 41-0236-3

La Collection®

Società per la Storia e l'Immagine dell'Automobile
I-20125 Milano, via Ponte Seveso 25

PRINTED AND BOUND IN ITALY
by Grafiche Editoriali Padane, Cremona, March 1992.

LAMBORGHINI DIABLO

Stefano Pasini

AUTOMOBILIA

INTRODUCTION TO PROJECT 132

When in June of 1985 the nod was given to design a new top-of-the-line Lamborghini to replace the Countach, the most important specification dictated by Emile Novaro and Patrick Mimran for the new flagship was extremely concise: apart from satisfying the indispensable requirements for a Lamborghini in terms of styling, luxury and exclusivity, the new car particularly had to be the fastest series production automobile in the world.

This was considered essential to endow this flagship of Sant'Agata with a comfortable margin in performance and image, which commercial director Ubaldo Sgarzi regarded as essential, even though this meant building a car that could exceed 315 kph, perhaps shooting for 200 mph as a nice round number in the world of British units of measure (330 kph). Of course, it also had to have suitable road manners and meet safety standards, but this went without saying for the Lamborghini technical staff, which immediately began studying the project.

By the end of 1985, some important decisions had already been made for delineating the basic makeup of the new car: the project was set down so that it would totally incorporate the successful formula of its illustrious forerunner but add some improvements, some suggested over the many years of Countach production and some demanded by the plethora of new international regulations, and with all the refinements made possible by the giant strides in technological progress. The mechanical scheme of the Countach was thus left untouched: the time-tested concept of the longitudinal, rear-mounted V-12 engine with the gearbox in front of it, anchored to a spaceframe.

The new Lamborghini was internally designated "Project 132", and the engineering design work was quickly initiated along these general guidelines with a technical team lead by Luigi Marmiroli, former designer for the Ferrari Racing Department and Alfa Romeo Formula 1.

We should bear in mind that in the early

When project 132 was set up it had a definite objective: to build a car which could take the 200 mph barrier and go faster than the Ferrari F40.

The 1988 "Anniversary" was the last version of the Countach. A limited series was produced to celebrate Lamborghini's 25 years' activity.

months of this project, part of the technical staff at Sant'Agata continued to perfect the Countach, both to make it more "reasonable" in its latter years of production life (work which led in 1988 to the Anniversary) and to evaluate the possibilities of evolving its design even further so that the Lamborghini supercar of the '90s could be extrapolated from it. They soon realized, however, that the increasingly stringent homologation standards made it virtually impossible to prolong the life of the Countach beyond 1990, so all they could do was restyle it to make its final years even more glorious.

Assigned full-time to this complex operation of plastic surgery on the Countach was Giulio Alfieri, then technical director of Lamborghini. His studies led to the design of an interesting "asymmetrical" Countach, later translated into a one-off prototype, that had some interesting feature (the thermostatic control on the side louvers was a fine idea) but was unfortunately too expensive and heavy to be seriously considered for just two-three years of series production. The car was later completed personally for Patrick Mimran and subsequently sold in Japan.

Thus the Countach Quattrovalvole was updated with a limited number of modifications (the Anniversary), while absolute priority was given to design work on the totally new automobile, entrusted to Marmiroli, who from then on became the true mentor of the 132. One reason was that increasingly stringent international regulations specifying the maximum allowable levels of chemical and noise pollution were creating major homologation problems for the glorious but dated structure of the Countach. Moreover, another problem, perhaps marginal but certainly not insignificant, was looming on the horizon: the car's roominess.

The Countach, as a great supercar, offered the driver and passenger little in terms of comfort, and some of its defects were intolerable on an automobile projected into the '90s. Naturally, no one at Sant'Agata ever thought Lamborghini should produce a driver-friendly car like a Porsche, but a course correction was certainly necessary toward more democratic driving, to permit the Bolognese flagship to be used by persons other than thin, athletic young men of average height. In a '90s perspective, in other words, they needed to think about selling to the tall, the chubby and the sedentary as well. These are the categories that have never been targeted by rear-engine Lamborghinis, from the Miura on. The project was thus formulated from the very outset with the firm idea in mind that the Type 132 had to offer not only absolute excellence in performance and formidable new styling but also good leg- and headroom, acceptable visibility even in the rear (an eternal flaw of the Countach) and some small unavoidable amenities such as side windows that open and an efficient climate-control system. With these specifications well in mind, Marmiroli launched into the design of the new car. Patrick Mimran and Emile Novaro gave the nod for its construction in early 1986.

The Diablo photographed in the factory yard. The futuristic designs of the Lamborghini cars has meant that they tend to suit unusual colours: the Miura for example was known for its distinctive orange colour, and the same is true of the Diablo, here in bright yellow.

Since the basic idea was thus to create a supercar that would generally reproduce the formula of its illustrious predecessor, with all the modifications deemed necessary and/or desirable, Luigi Marmiroli's technical team set instantly to work on the new Project 132. To appreciate the workload of Lamborghini's engineers at the time, we must remember that in the initial phase of gestation the 132 project was followed by a small group, while another part of the Sant'Agata technical staff was pursuing development on the LM all- terrain vehicle and the Jalpa, another continued to refine the Countach to make it more "reasonable" in its final years of production life (work which led to the Anniversary in 1988) and a small team was developing Alfieri's Countach.

In any event, work on Project 132 began vigorously, and a problem become immediately evident that was to become almost the pivotal point of the whole story of the new Lamborghini, or at least its most troublesome, controversial chapter: the body design. Not surprisingly, since it was a Lamborghini, the question of lines was immediately assigned top priority. It was no mystery for anyone, in fact, that the secret of the Countach's long success was linked more to its extraordinary bodywork than its performance, so one of the first concerns for everyone was to find the right "hand" for the task. Curiously, in the turmoil of this choice, there was a sort of flashback to that faroff 1963 when Ferruccio Lamborghini was seeking the person who could make "the right shoe for his foot".

If for so many years the best things from Lamborghini had been the product of intense collaboration with the atelier of Nuccio Bertone (e.g. Miura, Espada, Urraco, Jarama, Silhouette and, of course, Countach), now things were significantly different. The brain behind the lines of those magnificent creations, Marcello Gandini, had left the Grugliasco firm to undertake a brilliant career as a free- lancer from his hermitage at Almese, and the

One of Gandini's greatest merits was that of reconciling his creative genius with the functional requirements which inevitably bind the design of a car like the Diablo. The air intakes for example: there are no less than eight, but they are integrated perfectly into the design without making it heavy.

Sketches highlighting the car's silhouette and outer volumes.

new styling boss at Bertone, Deschamps of France, had been somewhat unconvincing with his remake of the Silhouette, which became the Jalpa. Even the dream car portfolio of the firm was rather scant at the time, so Lamborghini decided not to assign Bertone the job, as many had presumed, but to take a look around.

Not that there was much to choose from, since Pininfarina was still closely tied to Ferrari (more flashes of 1963) and so many other genial designers in the '60s and '70s, including Ghia, Zagato, Touring and Marazzi, had declined or even disappeared. Even the shining star of Italian coach design of the moment, Giorgetto Giugiaro, was contacted by Lamborghini but proposed nothing more than a bland reworking of his "Etna" proposal (destined for Lotus, and quite similar to an Elite), which was quickly set aside, as were other proposals cultivated in-house. The choice of stylist thus returned, with no possibility of doubt, to Gandini, a choice that must have satisfied everyone: on the one hand, those who knew and appreciated his fine current talents and, on the other, those who had remained enamoured of his extraordinary past creations.

So the genial Piedmontese designer was commissioned to conceive and present (overnight, naturally) an automobile that would adorn the 132's mechanicals so as to create a worth heir to the Countach, while bearing in mind the need for greater practicality and better aerodynamic efficiency, which constituted the other basic requisites of the new car. When Marcello Gandini presented his ideas only a few weeks later, everyone saw that the "Maestro" had once again hit the nail on the head.

Whatever the case, once he was assigned the job, Gandini set to work with his usual rapidity to develop the design of "his" new Lamborghini, as he had been given a deadline only four months away. This was nothing extraordinary for the lightning-fast stylist, who had received an assignment from Bertone to body the chassis of the Lamborghini P400 in mid-November of 1965 and had delivered the completed prototype of the Miura at the beginning of March 1966, in time for the Geneva Auto Show.

With equal urgency, Marmiroli spurred his technical team on to define the characteristics of the 132 and start preparing the mechanical parts necessary to build an initial prototype. At the start of 1986 the general lines and (more importantly) the overall dimensions of Gandini's design were approved, and work on the first prototype began effectively on 5 June 1986. Luigi Marmiroli, at that point, had been assigned full-time to the creation of the new flagship (an assignment that resulted

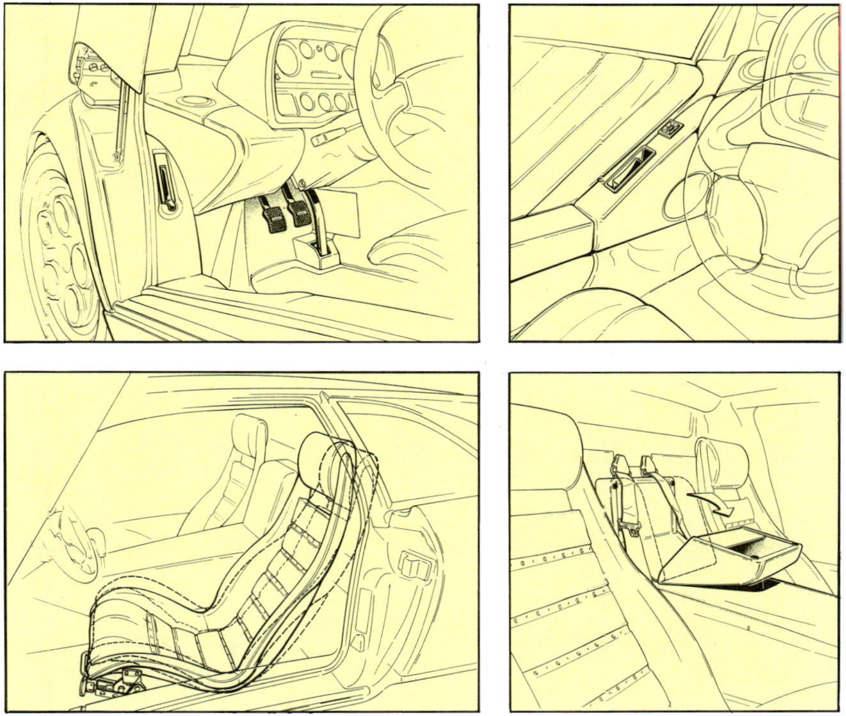

Top left, with the door open, the floor controls. Below, the rocker seat.

Top right, the controls on the left of the driver. Below, a fold up oddment container between the two seats.

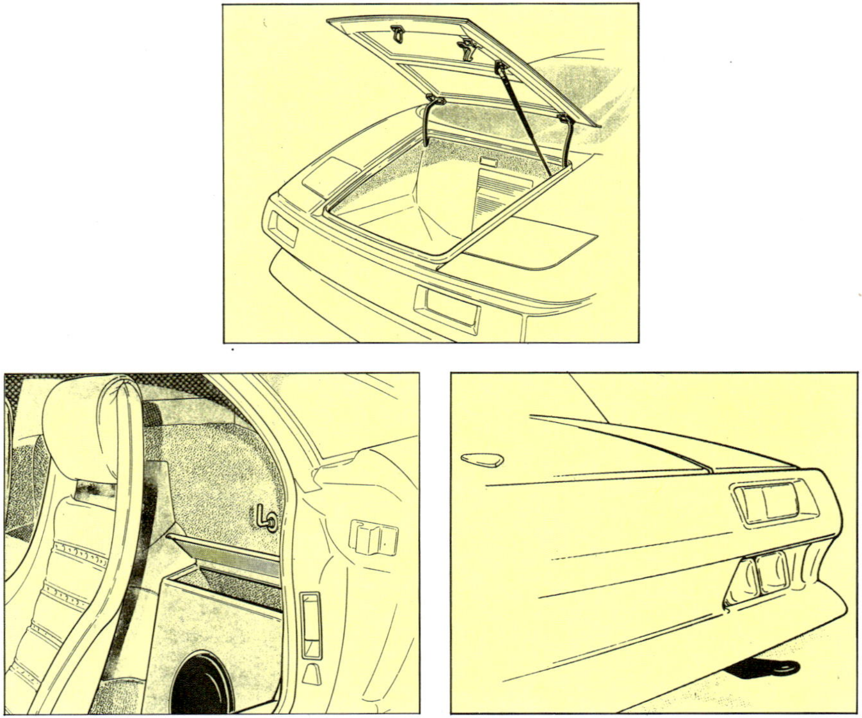

Three details in close-up: boot, odd-ment compartment, towing hook.

in numerous problems and misunderstandings between him and plant manager Giulio Alfieri).

To simplify the construction, it was decided to retain the Countach's tubular space frame but make it simpler by using fewer large boxed elements of chromium-molybdenum steel and thus a larger structural "web". The reason was not only to improve manufacturing simplicity but also to cut costs, facilitate repairs, provide greater access space through the tube network and reduce weight: at 80 kg it was 30 kg lighter than the Countach frame. The objective of making this frame simpler, lighter and more rugged than the preceding version was achieved by means of an in-depth study under Marmiroli's control at I FOA by Antonella Bertuzzi using a computer.

The classic 60° V-12 cylinder engine was retained, of course, but it was modified with respect to the Countach Quattrovalvole's 5167-cc version. Designated the "521", it was so extensively redesigned that it was considered all-new. It was lower and designed from the start to be equipped with the latest-generation electronic injection, with Weber- Marelli-Lamborghini components for controlling mixture, air and spark advance via specific memories at 16x8 and 16x10 points (the whole thing supervised and tested by Ceccarani), four valves per cylinder, 5.3

litres, over 460 HP (at least 30 more than the 5167-cc in K-Jetronic injection version) and up to 650 HP on the test bed.

The suspensions were completely redesigned and based on upper and lower quadrilaterals with anti-dive angle and dual rear shock-absorbers. For the brakes, parts from the Countach were adapted initially. From the construction of the first prototype they decided to introduce a system of four-wheel drive on the 132 as soon as possible, with the gearbox in front of the block and a third central differential and torque splitter (a mechanical group was specified initially) to provide 70% power on the rear axle and 30% in front.

Other technical themes they decided to develop for application on the 132, though with less urgency, were a possible ABS and an active suspension system. Of course, the problems that had continually plagued the Countach were attacked first in conceiving the new car. For example, to keep engine temperature under constant control, the radiators were designed with rather generous dimensions and were placed from the outset behind the engine block, to exploit an abundant air flow conveyed from below and laterally and thus reduce the dimensions of the unavoidable upper air scoop to the indispensable minimum (not warmly greeted by the technicians because of their lift effect). This flow

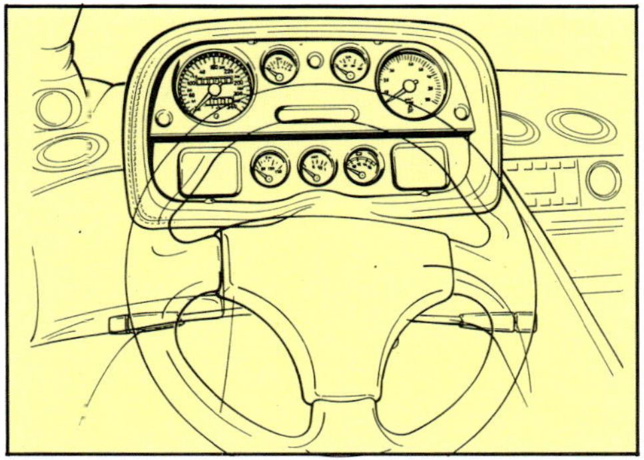

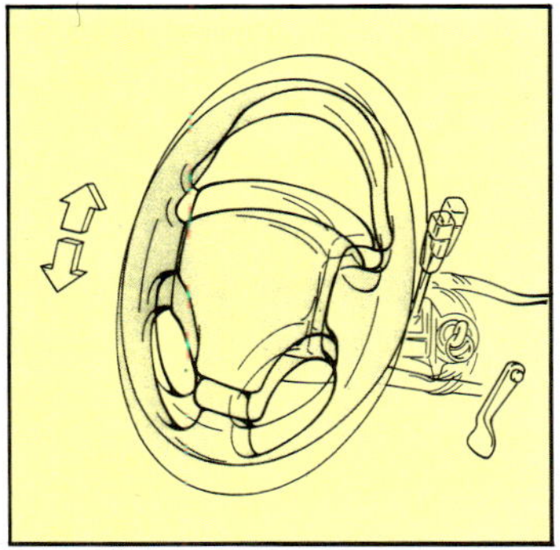

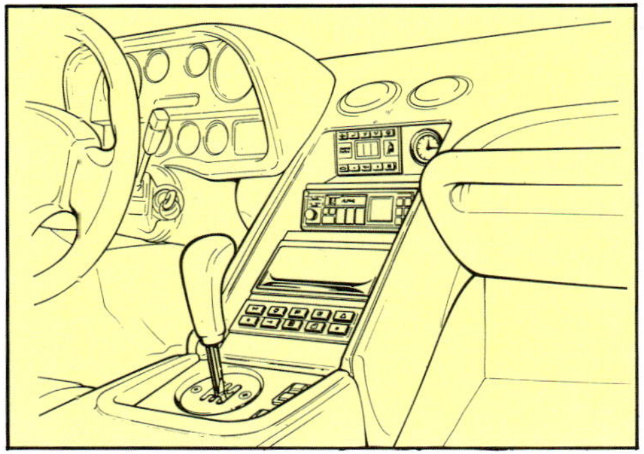

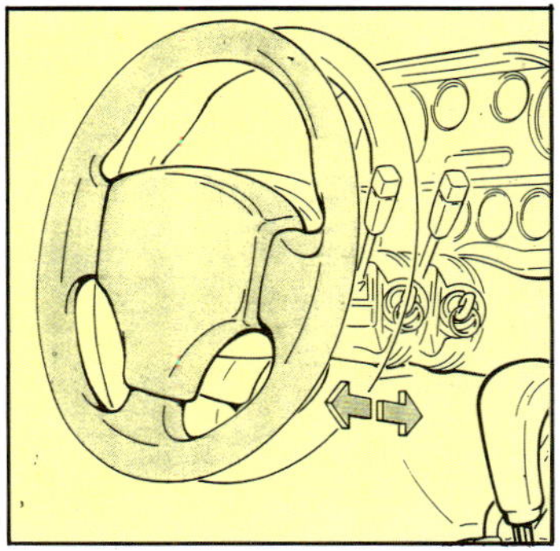

Top left, the dashboard: the instruments are not hidden by the wheel. Below, the centre console with stepped controls, and the gear lever.

Top right, the adjustable steering wheel. Below, its positions against the dashboard.

was also promoted by an original air extractor/conveyor created to act as both wing and bumper at the bottom edge of the tail panel and masterfully incorporated into a body for which Gandini expressed the best of his ideas.

As prescribed in Lamborghini specifications, Gandini had devoted utmost attention to the aerodynamics of all the surfaces, proposing flush-mounted glass, rounded forms, experimental wipers that stowed away under a pannel at the base of the windshield, an integrated chin spoiler, vertically-opening doors with generous window area characterized by a "drooping" line in front and full-lowering glass and hideaway headlamps with small "eyelid" openings. Of course the 132 was a straight two-seater, quickly endowed with a generous luggage compartment little hampered by the mandatory safety structures. The spare tyre and tools were initially to be accommodated in a lateral compartment accessible from the interior (to avoid placing a Bristol-style opening on the outside, which Gandini didn't like).

At the same time as the mechanical and bodywork design, a study of the interior was initiated, with special attention devoted to instrument legibility. With the consultation of Renato Meduri, professor of physiopathologic optics at the University of Bologna and researcher in the psychology of sight, it was decided to place the main instruments (speedometer, oil pressure, water temperature and especially the tachometer) outside the perimeter of the steering wheel, with the tachometer angled 8-10° right for high instinctive legibility even under extreme conditions (split-second perception of the needle position when driving at high speeds, unfavorable light conditions, etc.).

When the totally hand-crafted first prototype (chassis no. 12,000) was completed, the car was immediately seen as beautiful. It was undoubtedly the most beautiful car in the world, made the Countach look instantly ancient and made any competitor vanish by comparison. That first 132 looked like a jet fighter, even in its volume ratios: small, short, tapered, down-pointing nose and curved cockpit section, well forward, like a canopy. Behind the cockpit was the enormous mass of the tail section, which even visually suggested the idea of a large, powerful engine (the jets), broad, with tight, tidy, sculptured lines.

The first prototype was painted an impartial, neutral gray just a shade darker then the "air superiority gray" of the USAF's F-14s: it looked like a wingless Mig 29. Officially, Marmiroli said he had chosen the medium gray so he wouldn't be influenced by color in judging the shapes, as Battista Pininfarina wisely used to suggest. But he also had it done, in a subtle move, to underscore the new car's threatening, "military" look, its air of total road hegemony. The enthusiasm over the new super- Lamborghini spread rapidly among all those who had the privilege to see it upon completion.

The future of Lamborghini was heading in the right direction, and it was a genuine sense of emotional participation that led everyone to work with great alacrity in this magnificent project. But the car was still lacking a name, and a Lamborghini without an original, exciting name could not be taken seriously. Emile Novaro felt compelled to procure all the available books on tauromachy, bullfighting and bull breeding, in the hopes of finding something worthy of the Miuras, Marzals, Urracos and Jsleros of the past. After a long search, however, the result was not one name but a long list of candidates. Daniele Audetto, then in charge of external relations for the Bolognese firm, cleverly decided to have the right name selected by an in-house panel consisting of thirty-odd factory managers, important dealers and devoted customers, who had to choose their favorite name from a long and picturesque list. Just to give an idea of the suggestions, they were offered Bravo, Macho, Mucho, Picador, El Rey, Diablo, Raya, Rochio, Vuelta, Mira, Fulgor, and some other even more improbable suggestions. It was a delicate and difficult decision, complicated by the need to stay on a par with the founder's intuition. Ferruccio Lamborghini, in fact, had hit the bull's- eye in legendary terms in 1966 by naming his extraordinary rear-engine P400 sports coupé after the fearsome bulls of breeder Don Edoardo Miura (at the time, the two men didn't even know each other; the introductions came later). In addition to the crisp musicality of the name "Miura", in fact, these bulls offered precisely the threateningly professional image suited to the styling and performance of the Bolognese *berlinetta*, a dream-come-true for marketing people. At the end of the voting, the winning moniker was "Diablo", and it was surely an excellent choice.

The Diablo badge with the bull logo is placed on the rear grille, near the rear foglight.

16·11·'89

DEVELOPMENT OF THE DIABLO

Meanwhile, work was proceeding swiftly on completion of the prototype for initial testing. The 5.2-litre engine was mounted for the first time on 20 March 1987. The block fit fine, but there were space problems for the exhaust manifold for the front three cylinders of the left bank, so it was removed to modify the frame and the manifold. Two "Type 521" engines were completed initially, one to put in the prototype and the other already involved since Christmas 1986 in bed testing. From that moment, the 521 was run for around 200 hours at various speeds, with power up to 450 HP and various conditions, without the slightest problem.

To analyze the exhaust temperature, a sensor was mounted on the exhaust pipe of the fourth cylinder on the left bank; a Lambda probe was mounted on a manifold of the same bank. As is standard operating procedure at Lamborghini for engines in the development phase, a cannula was inserted in each of the 12 cylinders to measure the efficiency and emissions (CO, CO_2, unburned hydrocarbons, etc.) of the individual cylinders. Some emission problems were discovered immediately: not even electronic injection is completely immune from the problems of carburetors, though it has the advantage over them of much lower heat-evaporation of the hydrocarbons.

As development was proceeding on the mechanical parts, the bodywork was also evolving, in functional as well as purely esthetic terms, to improve its overall efficiency. To achieve this, as soon as the prototype was ready, with engine installed definitively on the chassis, complete with all accessories (27 March 1987) and provisional mounting of principal body parts and systems (electricals, etc.), it was immediately transported to a wind tunnel near Paris (considerations of secrecy excluded the use of similar Italian facilities).

Initial wind tunnel testing was then conducted from 29 to 31 March 1987. For this delicate transport job, the factory built a special trailer so that the 132, covered with

Certain details allow one to guess that this rendering by Chrysler stylist William Dayton is of the American version: the indicators are infact on the front and rear bumpers.

a tarpaulin, could be towed by a normal Volvo Station Wagon, without the use of a closed van. But this solution turned out to be unexpectedly risky, when the trailer proved so unstable that it caused the car to do a full spin on the tollway near Piacenza, during its Sant'Agata-Paris journey. Considering the risk run by that precious first prototype on that occasion, a van was used to transport the first 132 after that. Perhaps to console Marmiroli and co-workers for the scare experienced on the tollway, the 132 gave excellent results in the wind tunnel. From the aerodynamic standpoint, the car was already quite efficient and ready in this first version for road-testing.

Between the prototype's return from the wind tunnel and the first cautious testing, however, two events took place that were to have a significant effect on the car's development. More directly linked to the car itself was the selection of a name: in mid-April it was finally decided, based primarily on the outcome of the internal poll, to give Project 132 the name "Diablo", from the name of a famous fighting bull from the breeding farm of the Duke of Veragua, which on 11 July 1869 sustained a dramatic encounter with *torero* Jose de Larra, a.k.a. "El Chicorro".

Of greater importance, partly for the implications it would later have on the history of the car itself, was the acquisition of Lamborghini by Lee A. Iacocca's Chrysler Corporation, officialized on 23 April 1987 after weeks of secret negotiations. It is well to note that at his point the Diablo was virtually a complete car ready for an industrialization study, certainly more ready than the Miura or Countach had been at their unveilings. The project had reached a point, before departing for the wind tunnel, that Marmiroli had been able to drive the semi-finished car briefly behind the main factory building, while on 22 April 1987, the day before the official signing of the contract between Chrysler and Mimran for sale of the company, Patrick Mimran had taken the 132 for a short drive inside the factory, complete with celebrative toasts.

Lamborghini Automobili was acquired by the American group for a sum never officially announced but presumably close to 25 million dollars, rather a bargain, in other words. But the purchase price was only part of the investment planned by Chrysler, which in subsequent months began showing a serious expansion program for Lamborghini, investing several tens of millions of dollars to extend the covered area from 22,500 sq.feet in 1987 (there had been 17,500 in 1981) to around 25,000, hiring new personnel and creating new structures to improve plant operation, while maintaining a high level of quality.

Rear view of the Diablo. The design shows the definitive version of the car's details too.

The purpose was not only to lift car production from the 320 units of 1987 to the 400 of 1989, with a forecast for 500 Diablos/Countaches/LMs in 1990, but also to prepare for the major leap in size planned for 1992, and the arrival of the smaller "Type 140", intended to push production over 2,000 units yearly. The chance thus offered Lamborghini, thanks to these abundant investments, to utilize highly advanced equipment (autoclaves for composites, sealed chambers for pollution checks, sophisticated test beds of the highest level, etc.) thus excuses Detroit to some extent for certain later interference in the purely technical aspects of Lamborghini management, particularly in development of the Diablo project. Furthermore, to stress the steadfast nature of the Chrysler's commitment to finance anything from Lamborghini that could enhance the talents available, a few days after the announcement of the change in company ownership, another press conference was called to make an even more unexpected announcement: Lamborghini was entering the world of automobile racing in grand style, with the creation of an independent division called Lamborghini Engineering, administered by Daniele Audetto and under the technical direction of engineering genius Mauro Forghieri. Following its highly effective entry into offshore powerboating, which had resulted in a rich harvest of European and world titles, the Bolognese firm was also entering the field of autoracing, breaking a voluntary abstinence declared at its founding, and was beginning in grand style with the project for a 3.5-litre 12-cylinder aspirated engine to be furnished to a team involved in the world Formula One championship.

At that point of the story, the official presentation of the Diablo was scheduled for May 1988, on the occasion of a grand international rally called "Lamborghini Day", a typically pyrotechnical creation of Audetto (in collaboration with Sandro Munari, the greatest rally driver of all times, hired at the time by Lamborghini as a P.R. man) to unveil the Diablo during celebrations of the company's 25th anniversary. Audetto planned to have the car lowered from a helicopter, in the midst of the Lamborghinis gathered on the Santa Monica circuit at Misano. It was to have been set down beside the 350 GTV "Numero Uno", the first Lamborghini ever produced, then undergoing a complete restoration in Bologna at Romano Bernardoni's Emilianauto and scheduled to be finished and running by then. According to the plan, the rally participants (the devoted owners of other Lamborghinis) were to be granted the privilege of advanced booking: anyone reserving one would have been able to test-drive it on the track.

The road tests were begun in the second

The dashboard in this design by William Dayton is almost the definitive one, except for the steering wheel and the huge passenger grab handle.

15.6.89

P.132 EURO-INTERIOR.
8.NOV. 89

half of 1987, immediately after completion of the first running prototype. Since the latter half of April the 132 "number zero" had been taken to low-traffic tollway stretches, such as the Imola-Ravenna bypass, for preliminary testing. On those occasions, the car was disguised to look as much as possible like an evolution of the Countach, an idea for attracting less attention and possibly fooling the great professionals of photographic espionage (like Hans Lehmann).

After the first rapid road trial, in mid-May, the car was transferred with all its accessory structures to the Testing Department, to leave more elbow room for shaping the final model and give more freedom to those who had to develop the 132. The early testing was conducted at night, and initially they reached 200 kph on the highway to Funo, but from 15 May 1987 they began conducting these trials by day. On Monday, 1 June 1987, Lee Iacocca arrived for a rapid look at the factory as Chairman of the Chrysler Corporation and effective owner of Lamborghini. To appreciate the factory's current production and its competition, especially from a future viewpoint, he ordered a Countach Quattrovalvole, the 132 prototype and a Testarossa to be placed side by side. Iacocca's reaction to the full-scale model of the Diablo was highly positive: he termed it "terrific".

During the first weekend of June, Marmiroli transferred the team to Nardò for the first high-speed tests on that fast track, with Valentino Balboni at the wheel. The results of these tests were instantly positive: the 132 reached a top speed of 301 kph, in fact, clocked a full lap at an average of 296 kph and demonstrated perfect stability even at these extremes. It was so stable, in fact, that Balboni could release the steering wheel at 240 with no problems. The only important defect noted was the excessive heating of the engine oil after long use at high speeds: after a few miles at 290 kph the temperature rose to over 150°C, with a significant drop in pressure, while the other temperatures gave no problems. The test at Nardò thus ended with good results.

On the other hand, these good results were not yet those truly desired by Marmiroli and the rest of the Lamborghini management. True, the 132 had reached the significant goal of 301 kph, but the Countach Quattrovalvole properly tuned could reach that speed despite its much "shabbier" aerodynamics. And then the 132 had been tested in a still uncluttered version, with the large rear window clear, few air intakes, a smooth shape with little disturbance and thus seemingly more penetrating than the version that would go into production and thus face everyday life (assuming a Lamborghini can live such a

This design, five months older than the previous one, refers to the European configuration of the Diablo.

life). And also without the important handicaps in terms of weight, heat or power drop that would later be inevitably created by the mandatory cleaning of exhaust gases with catalytic converters, air pumps, etc. There was thus some concern at that point over achieving the principal goal they had set at the start of the project, i.e. obtaining a top speed well above that of any other production car. The prototype's 521 engine was immediately removed to look for problems, and then a restudy phase was declared to determine why the car overheated and performed below desired levels. For the temperature, the problems could be easily resolved: eliminate the enormous rear window that held in so much heat and increase the size of the oil coolers, fans and air scoops, all routine operations. But all this would cause a great increase in wind drag, greater friction, greater weight. So a more drastic solution was required, and Marmiroli, after a thorough discussion with Lamborghini Chairman Emile Novaro, decided to attack the problem at its roots, by simply injecting more horsepower and torque through a new larger and more powerful engine. This gave rise to the "522" engine project. The gestation period of the 132 was beginning to lengthen.

It was difficult to speed up the development process significantly, due in part to simple personnel problems. As we said earlier, the work capacity at Lamborghini was not channeled entirely to the 132. At the same time the rather pure experimental work continued. In this area Marmiroli, appointed technical director after the departure of Giulio Alfieri, and truly the key man in the Diablo project, had already decided in 1986 to test the possibility of using composite materials in constructing a high-performance automobile for road use, to develop experience that could be applied in constructing the Diablo.

At the end of 1987, the factory began to realize that it couldn't realistically have the Diablo ready by the end of the following year, primarily because of all the modifications the new ownership was beginning to "suggest" for the Bolognese flagship with respect to the plain basic Marmiroli/Gandini design. But then the Quattrovalvole had to be replaced, if not by a radically new automobile at least by a more refined, civil model that would bring the Countach era to a glorious end, within the evolutionary process that had characterized that supercar. For this reason, the perfected version of the Quattrovalvole was unveiled in September 1988 at the same "Lamborghini Day" when the Diablo was to be announced.

The Anniversary, as the new Countach was named to underscore the fact that it was being produced in the 25th year of the company's existence, revealed little of the teachings of the legendary Evoluzione nor the advanced research on the Diablo. It was, in effect, a much refined special edition of the Countach, upgraded with a more conventional interior, an efficient climate-control system, electric window-lifts and other such amenities. The exterior denoted a clear attempt to make the car's line more streamlined and tidier with smoother blending of spoiler and wheel houses, while the magnificent built-up O.Z. wheels made their appearance to accommodate the extraordinary Pirelli P-Zero tyres. This new edition also aroused considerable interest among customers, and in effect it was a notable commercial success for Lamborghini, with a flood of orders bearing delivery dates several months in the future. It was clear to all that this was to be the last evolution of the series and that the Diablo was about to arrive (although most, in 1988, hoped they would not have to wait two more years to see it on the market).

Naturally, the Anniversary was a palliative, though a luxurious one, and while the indominable Ubaldo Sgarzi could only grin at its success, he also understood that with competitive pressure growing stronger by the day, the Diablo was to become the key to Lamborghini's future: and the sooner it came out, the better. He was not alone in feeling some concern over the Diablo in those early months of 1988: the story of the new car, at this point, had suddenly become rather complicated. In June of 1987, in fact, the 132 had already been the subject of an in-depth examination by the new management. Iacocca, as we said, had publicly described it as "terrific", but meanwhile his colleagues were already thinking otherwise.

The Diablo's body on its way to the complex paint phase.

The skirmishing that followed in the succeeding months, apparently focused on "suggestions" for small detail modifications, were in reality attempts to slow down the crystallization process of the de-

A Diablo ready for the MIRA tests, painted the usual blue.

finitive car so that an alternative all-American line could be proposed, to the greater glory of the Design Center in Detroit. In mid-June a Chrysler designer, evidently authorized from on high, handed Gandini, Marmiroli and Guerra a sketch with proposed modifications to the 132, that would bring the car closer to the Countach, without detaching itself radically as in the original design (so much for Lamborghini's innovative traditions...).

At the end of that same month, a set of photos of the interior of the prototype were taken to Detroit so that the Design Center could express its views. Things were looking bad for a highly Italian Diablo. To complicate things even further, a serious road accident in the summer of that same 1987 seriously threatened the life of Emile Novaro. The charismatic chairman of Lamborghini was driving the tollway to Monte Carlo in his Audi 200 Quattro at over 200 kph when a large dog crossed the road in front of him. In an attempt to avoid the animal, Novaro lost control of the car, which rolled over several times and plummeted down a ravine. Miraculously alive, Novaro remained on the critical list for several days due to multiple fractures throughout his body, lacerations of some internal organs and cuts and bruises all over. Only his tough fiber enabled him to survive such a dramatic accident, but he was still confined to a hospital bed for several weeks, unable to follow events at Sant'Agata. Much of the staff, after breathing a sigh of relief that their chairman had survived (he had become a legendary figure inside the Bolognese firm), began to realize that his absence could have some highly undesirable effects. And so it did.

Novaro's accident deprived Lamborghini of leadership, and the forced absence of the man who had actively worked to retain his company's independence from its American owners favored the intensification of urgent requests from various sources for changes in the Diablo's lines. In any case, because of these pressures, the Diablo began to undergo an endless series of transformations. The idea of the young "talents" at Chrysler, who wanted to make the 132 a caricature of the Countach, was naturally rejected. The design was handed back to Gandini, who took the right half of the original 132 model, painted red, and used it to prepare a new proposal, creating a characteristic asymmetrical mockup of the Diablo.

In October of 1987, Gandini managed to present his second proposal for the 132, that right half of the red mockup divided longitudinally into two parts for treatment of the front end and especially the rear. The left half (drivers's side in Italy) was the same as the original design, while the right showed a general softening effect. It, too, was quite handsome, in effect, perhaps lacking just a bit of the innovative flair of the former. During its transformation toward the production version, as was clearly evident in the asymmetrical mockup, this second version of the 132 had become less aggressive, because it was less angular and had more glass area. On the whole, judging from the mockup, the new 132 was becoming extremely handsome, though more complex, softer in front and more intricate in the rear than the first version, generally attractive though less clean-cut, but still extremely Lamborghini.

To put it simply, the situation at the end of 1987 was not particularly encouraging: the first car, when it reached the functional prototype stage, had been rejected and demoted to the role of testing backup car; the second (stillborn in the form of that famous asymmetrical mockup) was criticized and basically rejected because, according to Iacocca, it was too "busy", i.e. too intricate, in the tail section. And while Maestro Gandini was patiently preparing another mockup based on the front end of the second prototype and seeking to design a more inoffensive rear end, the American stylists, having had time to work, began sending no longer simple "suggestions" but entire clay models to be transported on the date established for a final decision on the Diablo's styling, around the end of January 1988.

During early 1988, therefore, development work went rapidly forward, seeking the best compromise to finalize the overall design of the Diablo, gradually translated into a single overall homogeneous picture worthy of the Lamborghini marque, thanks in part to the improved conditions of Emile Novaro. Once he was off the critical list, the chairman began a long period of convalescence, gradually intensifying his appearances at Sant'Agata precisely so he could follow project 132 more closely, picking up the reins of "his" company and supporting the appeals of his technicians

The engine with longitudinal gearbox. Its compactness is at the limit of compatibility with the capacity. Both cylinder heads and crankcase are in light aluminium alloy. The photograph was taken in the factory in conditions which were not ideal, as can be seen from the two bricks acting as a support.

after the ambiguous situations experienced the year before. Perhaps it was just a coincidence, but in mid-1988 a further proposal by Gandini, approved by the Italian management, was also judged totally suitable to the expectations of Lamborghini for its flagship. The front end was taken from the second design, the tail had been cleaned up and some of the lines judged too transgressive for refined palates had been softened. The approved Diablo form was rather soft but still svelte and attractive. It had lost the aggressiveness – half-starship half-Group C two-seater – that had made the Countach a success, but it followed the general trend to use curvier lines, more efficient from the aerodynamic standpoint (and less risky in their impact on the public). At this point the work of designers, stylists and creative geniuses was over. It was time for the engineers who would develop the project to pinpoint hidden defects, perfect details and put it into production.

In the meantime, the first backup of the 132 (chassis no. 12000) had circulated extensively, and not always in secrecy. This was the version based on the boxed-member frame, with a 521 engine and Gandini's original bodywork with its vast rear window covering the engine, still in the usual mute gray with no camouflage, the one that had been photographed and published in the major motoring magazines. Less known was the fact that the new 522 engine, with 5.7 litres and over 500 HP, created, as we have seen, to raise the Diablo's performance above all the competition, had been completed and was already running full tilt under the innocent clothing (innocent?) of a Quattrovalvole of the testing department, putting on a demonstration of speed and efficiency. Much essential data was collected from this mobile laboratory before the 522 was then installed in the second Diablo prototype (with the bodywork built according to Gandini's third design, chassis no. 12001, dark gray in color, in all respects the first prototype of the definitive version). Only when this second backup car was completed with the 5.7-litre engine could the car be placed on the road in its quasi-final version for real testing. And then the world's major automotive magazines were able to publish photographs of the updated Diablo, which barring a few minor modifications was already the one earmarked for production.

During 1989, progress on the Diablo went steadily forward, and many details had to be further updated, modified and perfected during the delicate process of finalizing the specifics of the car to be placed into series production, the preparation of homologations for the entire world, etc. Thus in this period the Diablo also acquired those final brushstrokes

Transverse section of the engine. A detail of the combustion chamber geometry: the cylinder heads are trapezoidal and the pistons concave.

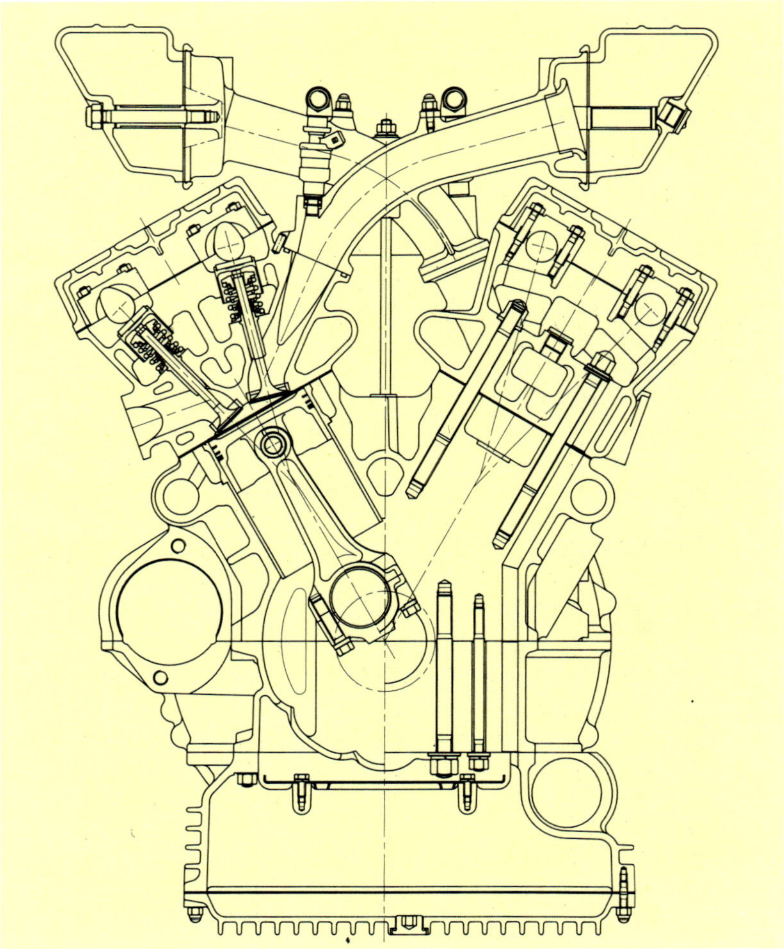

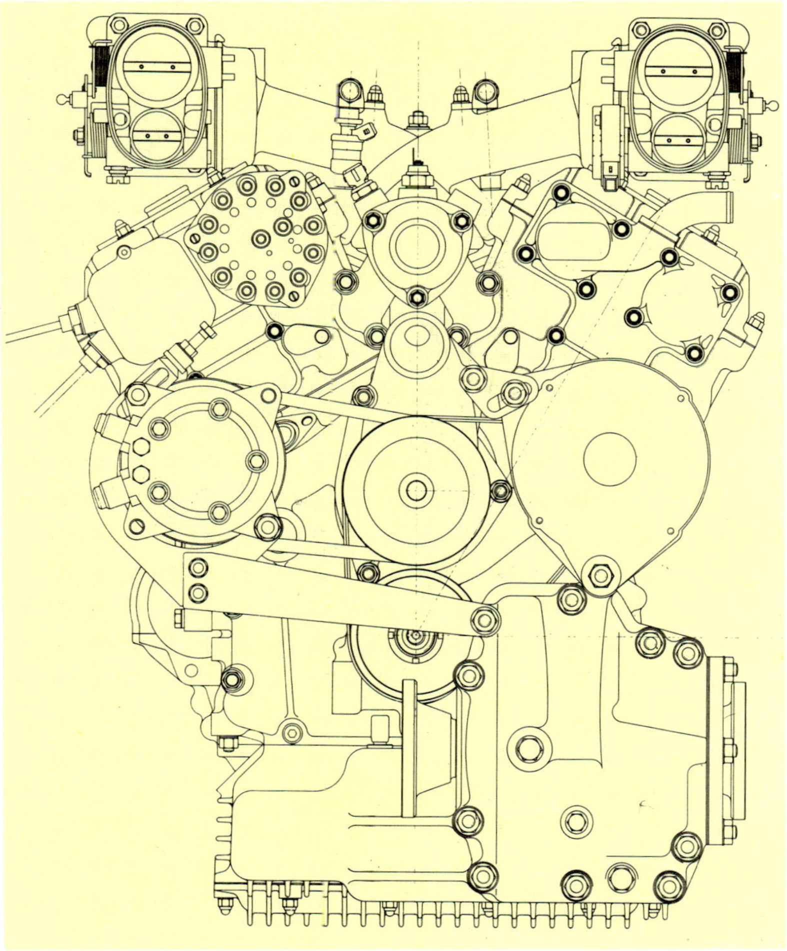

Frontal view of the engine in an official Lamborghini technical drawing.

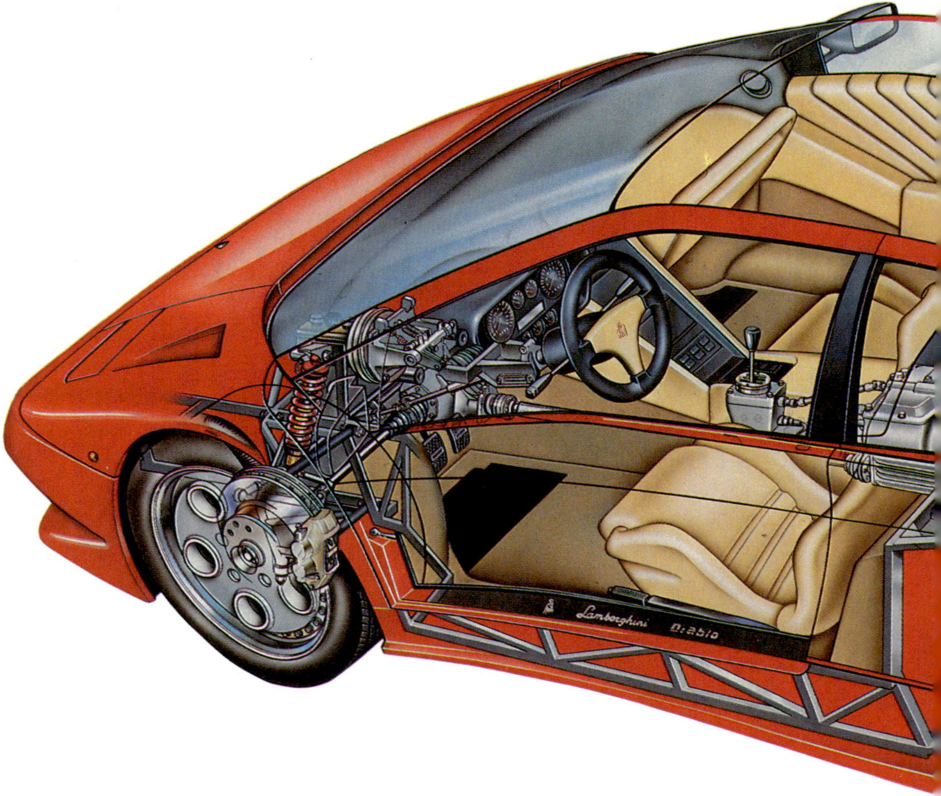
Lamborghini
Diablo

Section of the Diablo by Anderlini. Note the cooling system with twin rear radiators in aluminium and the big laterally-sited tank.

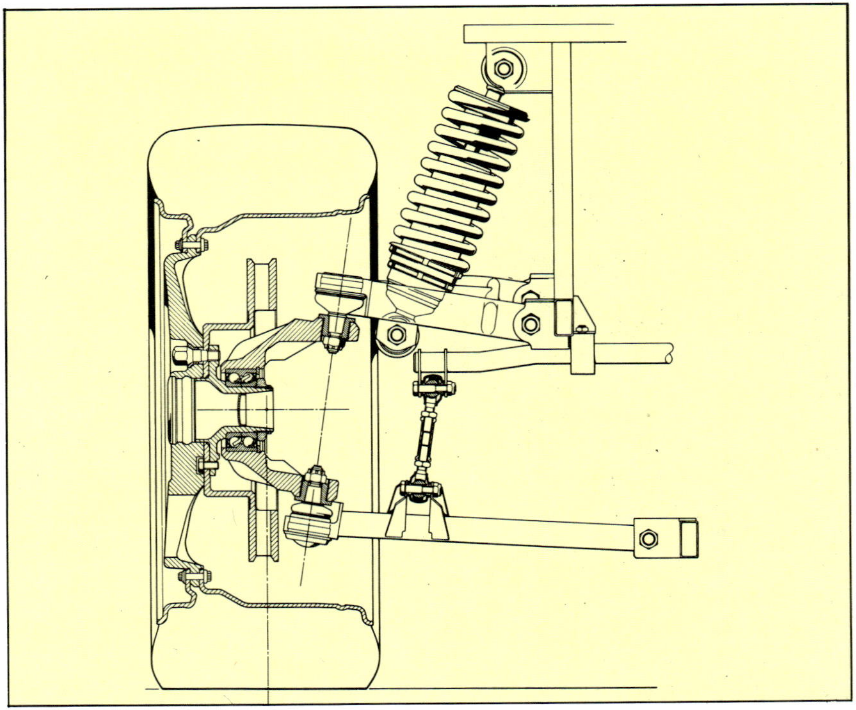

Transverse section of the front suspension with a single coil on the same axis as the damper and anti-dive geometry.

which had been left up in the air during the stylistic feuding between Italy and the U.S.

As we have seen, it had been decided from the early inception of the project, though with some reluctance, to permanently abandon carburetors in favor of a highly efficient Weber- Marelli-Lamborghini fuel-injection system to improve emission quality, an extremely important factor, considering the large number of Diablos they hoped to distribute in countries such as Switzerland, California and Japan, wealthy but traditionally rigid in term of anti-pollution legislation. An extremely important innovation in this sophisticated system was the significant contribution of Lamborghini itself to the design of the entire system, not purchased "off the shelf" from outside firms but minutely specified by the engineers of the Bolognese firm, particularly Ceccarani, especially on the software side.

From the mechanical standpoint, the need to hasten the Diablo to the production phase caused a temporary postponement of studies on four-wheel drive. The system based on a central mechanical differential, initially included by Marmiroli, had already been excluded by the decision to utilize a central viscous coupling along the line of the Ferguson systems, hence the designation chosen for the 4WD version ("VT" for "viscous traction"). The need to concentrate all efforts on the "normal" car thus caused the 4WD version to be put on a back burner. In the same manner, the pace of development was slowed on the semi-automatic clutch, necessitated by specific demands of the North American market. The Fichtel & Sachs system was rejected, while evaluations continued on the excellent similar system produced by Valeo.

To meet the rigorous licensing standards, the rear and front lighting groups were changed, many detail modifications were made to bumpers and safety structure in view of the painful but inevitable crash test. At the MIRA, Diablo prototype number 12004, painted an inevitable opaque light blue, was hurled against the barrier with excellent results in terms of impact absorption and dissipation. Considering the enormous kinetic energy and momentum that such a large, heavy mid- rear engine exerts on the cockpit cell in the event of a frontal impact, the degree of resistance of that cell left even the technicians of the British institute pleasantly surprised. This resistance obviously translates into excellent protection for the car's occupants in the unfortunate event of a collision.

In addition to passive safety, the so-called "active" variety (i.e. the ability of the car to collaborate with the driver to actively avoid an accident, as opposed to its ability to passively minimize its negative effects) was improved through a

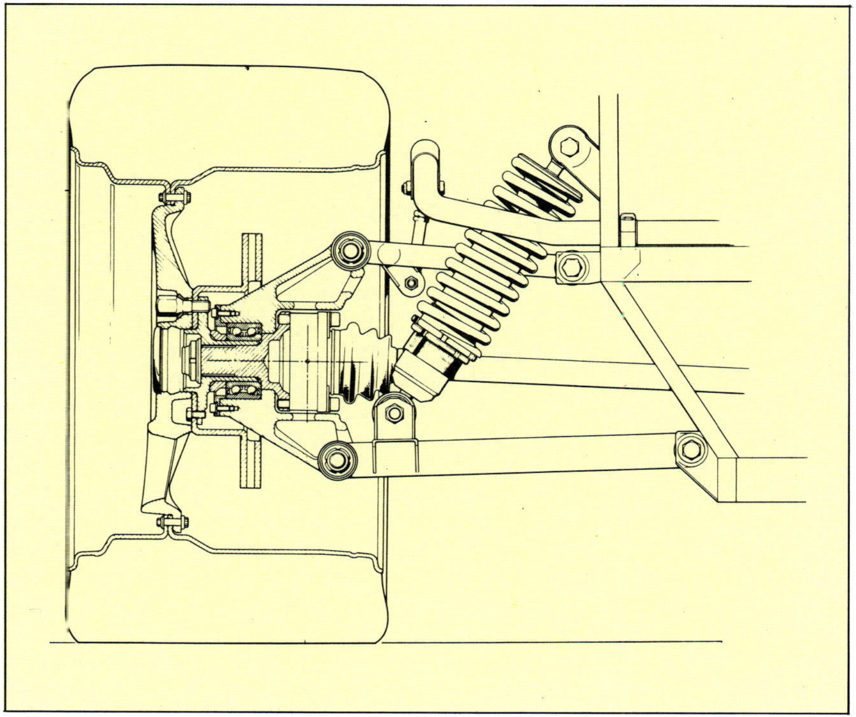

Transverse section of the rear suspensions with twin coils, coaxial dampers and anti-squat geometry.

meticulous job of refinement: many modifications of this type were suggested by Sandro Munari, outstanding superfast test-driver, who insisted on the need to update the cooling of the brake discs and other chassis details with respect to the features of the Countach to fit the performance of these systems to the Diablo's 500 horses and thus improve its overall quality both in road use, and in rarer but certainly probable racetrack use. The exceptional efficiency and fatigue resistance of the Diablo's new braking system are thus noteworthy, not only compared to past Lamborghini production but also with respect to all the other top-level supercars. A more efficient system was created for channeling fresh air to the brake discs. It was also decided to eliminate the spare tyre. This drastic decision was reached after reflecting that in effect the main problem of a flat tyre on a Countach was not so much restoring enough pressure to drive on, which can be achieved temporarily (even on the big P7s) with a couple of flat-repair bottles, but the impracticality of removing one of these bulky tyres and then having to haul it around in the only available realistic place, i.e. the passenger seat (or passenger's lap).

The delays generated by stylistic problems inevitably led the plant managers to push development with all-out urgency, once they finally got the go-ahead for production, which was not a sure thing until mid-1989. The formidable problems always associated with the industrialization of such a supercar were obviously amplified by the need to conform to rigid international homologation standards, by the ever-improving quality level of the competition and by the need to match up components most of which were new to Lamborghini.

One point of controversy in finalizing the "series" Diablo was the design of the cockpit interior. Gandini, famous for his clamorous bodystyling creativity, has never shown enthusiasm over interior designing, and up to that point the cockpit had only been rough-sketched, along the general lines of previous Lamborghinis, with the innovation of the new dashboard but without other improvements. The ownership thus decided to send an American designer to Sant'Agata to organize the cockpit and dashboard project with an industrial mentality.

The dashboard, which was already "two-level" in the no. 12000 (accessory instruments and warning lights below, steering wheel, tachometer and speedometer/odometer above) was redesigned to become a large console with the instruments dispersed in such a way that they could be read inside and outside the steering-wheel ring. It was designed to be highly unadorned, with elimination of the glove compartment (replaced by a compartment between the seatbacks).

On the door-liners, the leather was placed in an unusual way for a Lamborghini, in diagonal strips, and the armrests become more conventional than the concealed handle on the Countach.

Almost to underscore the less sporty, more comfortable quality of the interior, the stereo system was studied with special care in the factory, and Alpine (firm whose association with Lamborghini had never lost its proper connotation of seeking the maximum regardless of cost) decided to prepare an authentic showroom of its best creations, also benefitting from the efficient new soundproofing applied on the Diablo.

The organization of the new structures for construction of the Diablo was confronted with decision between 1989 and 1990. The main building, where the Jalpa and Countach were built, would be used for assembling the mechanical parts, upholstering, painting and initial mounting of the bodywork on the chassis (also produced outside), and these operations, along with machining of the rough castings and quality control, occupied practically all the space available in that building. Finishing and completion of the Diablo, with all the followup road-testing, were transferred to a new building behind the first, to gain space and streamline work for everyone. The quarters of the Spare Parts Service of the precious Customer Service Division was left on the other side of the main roadway, next to the fast-growing Testing Department with its new laboratories. Once the green light had been given more or less clearly to the final configuration of the Diablo, at some point in 1989, the pace of work became frenetic. With designing on the P 140 10-cylinder still in the early stages, the Jalpa long suspended and the LM in a demobilization phase, only the Diablo was left to sustain Lamborghini, beginning as soon as possible.

The tubolar steel chassis is very light and has very high torsional resistance.

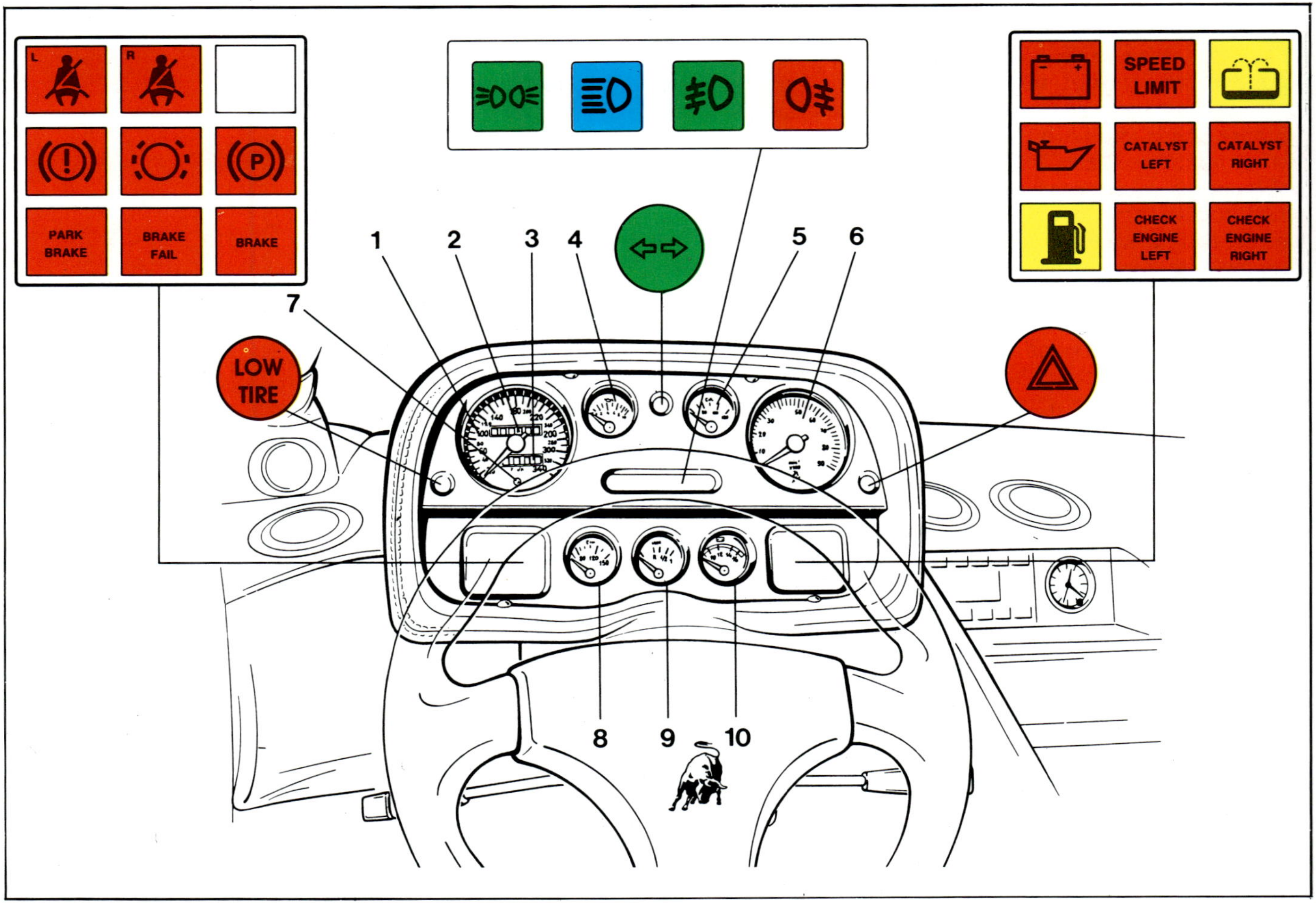

L
R
PARK BRAKE
BRAKE FAIL
BRAKE
SPEED LIMIT
CATALYST LEFT
CATALYST RIGHT
CHECK ENGINE LEFT
CHECK ENGINE RIGHT
LOW TIRE
1
2
3
4
5
6
7
8
9
10

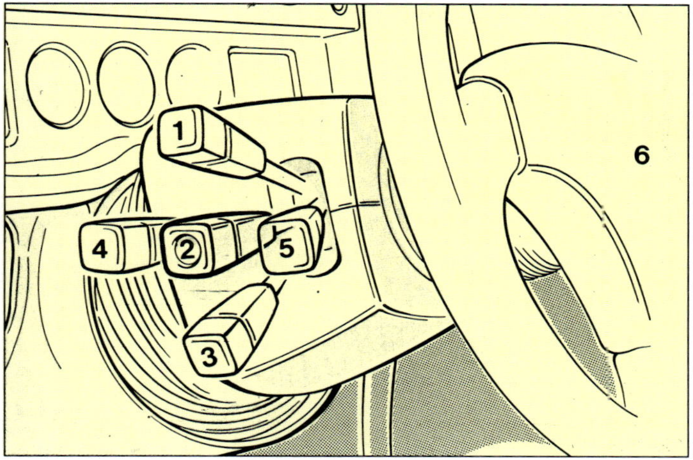

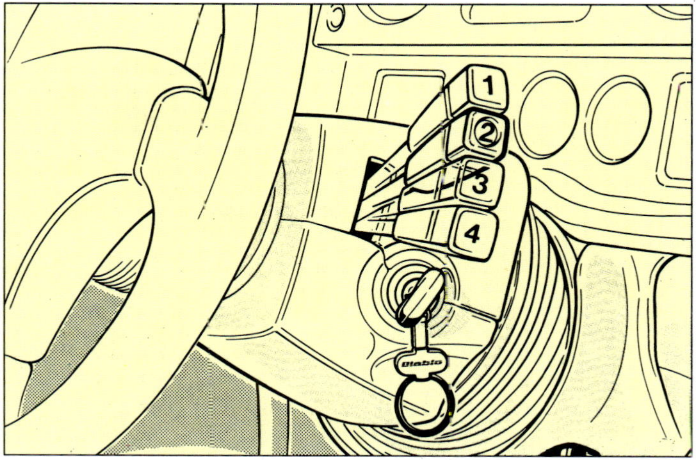

Left-hand page: instruments and warning lights.

1. Speedometer
2. Odometer
3. Trip meter
4. Oil pressure gauge
5. Water temperature gauge
6. Tachometer
7. Trip reset
8. Oil temperature gauge
9. Fuel level
10. Battery tension gauge

Top, left: the light control lever

1. Turn to right
2. Off
3. Turn to left
4. High beam
5. Day flash

Top, right: the windscreen wiper

1. Wiping
2. Off
3. 1st speed
4. 2nd speed

ENGINE

Disposition: central longitudinal
Materials: light alloy cylinder head and crankcase
Cylinders: V12 60°
Bore and stroke: 87x80 mm (3.425x3.149 in)
Piston displacement: 5707 cc (348.41 cu in)
Compression ratio: 10:1
Maximum power: 362 kW (492 HP) at 6800 rpm
Maximum torque: 580 Nm (57 kgm) at 5200 rpm
Timing system: double overhead camshaft, 4 valves per cylinder
Injection and ignition: electronic sequential multipoint, type Lamborghini LIE
Lubrication: dry sump
Cooling system: double rear radiator
Emission control system: 3-way catalytic converters and lambda sensors

DRIVELINE

Drive: rear-wheel
Clutch: dry single-plate
Gearbox: manual, 5-speed + Rev
Gear ratios: 1st= 2.312, 2nd= 1.524, 3rd= 1.125, 4th= 0.888 5th= 0.676, Rev= 2.125
Final ratio: 2.410
Differential: self-locking

CAR BODY

Type: 2-door sports coupe, 2 seats. Design by Marcello Gandini
Frame: steel alloy tubes integrated with sections in composite materials
Front suspensions: independent wheels, A-arms, coaxial spring shock absorbers
Rear suspensions: independent wheels, A-arms, 2 coaxial spring shock absorbers
Steering system: rack and pinion, Ø13.2 m
Brakes: ventilated discs, twin independent hydraulic system with booster
Rims: front 8½x17", rear 13Jx17"
Tyres: 245/40 ZR 17, rear 335/35 ZR 17
Fuel tank: 100 l (22 imp.gal.)

DIMENSIONS AND WEIGHTS:

Length: 4460 mm (175 in)
Width: 2040 mm (80 in)
Height: 1105 mm (43 in)
Wheelbase: 2650 mm (104 in)
Front and rear tracks: 1540/1560 mm (60 /64 in)
Kerb weight: 1686 kg (3746 lbs)
Luggage capacity: 141 dm^3 (5 cu ft)

PERFORMANCE

Top speed: 325 kph (202.3 mph)
Acceleration from 0 to 100 kph: 4.1 sec
1 km from standing start: 20.7 sec
Pick-up (in 5th gear from 70 to 120 kph): 9.8 sec
Speed per 1000 rpm (5th gear): 46.4 kph (28.89 mph)
Braking distance (140 kph): 72.6 m (79.78 yd)
Consumption at 90/120/Urban Cycle: 13.3/15.2/28.9 l/100 km
Pass-by noise (at 120 kph): 77.1 Db
Specific power: 86.2 HP/liter (1.41 HP/cu in)
Weight to power ratio: 3.4 kg/HP (7.61 lbs/HP)

NOTES: air conditioned, HI-FI system, electric windows, central locking as standard equipment

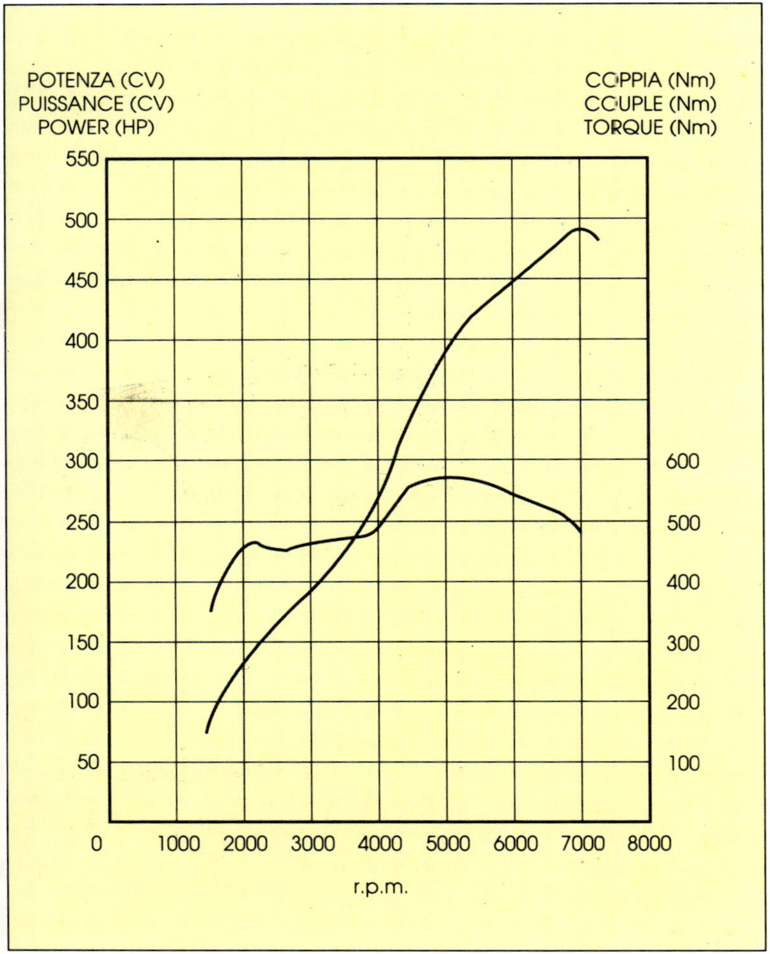

The power and torque curves of the Diablo 12-cylinder.

The wide range of colours in which the Diablo is available.

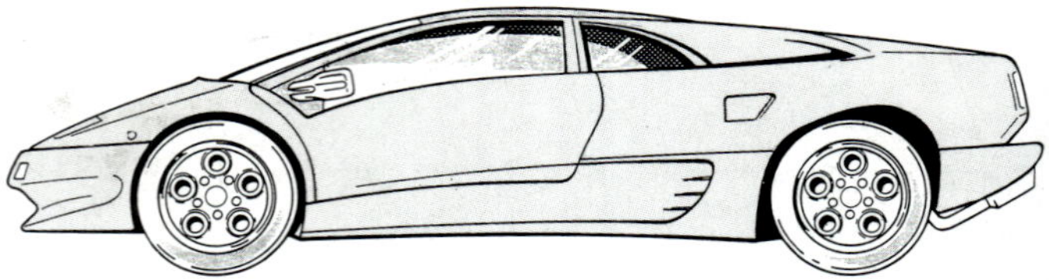

224.009 Ballon white met.

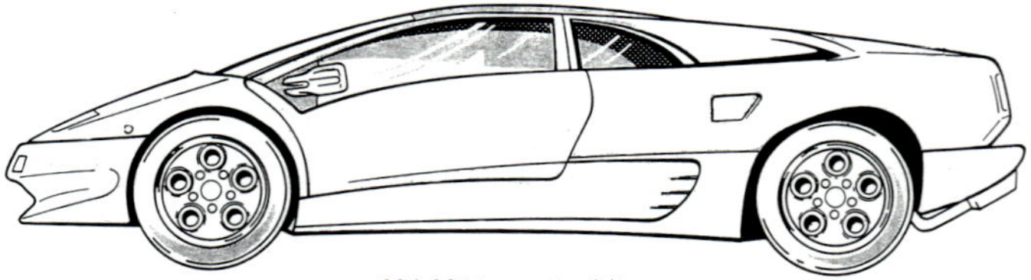

231.023 Impact white

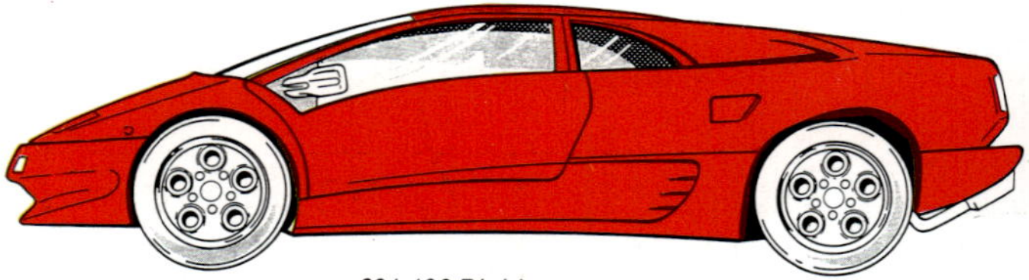

231.136 Diablo rosso

231.233 Super fly yellow

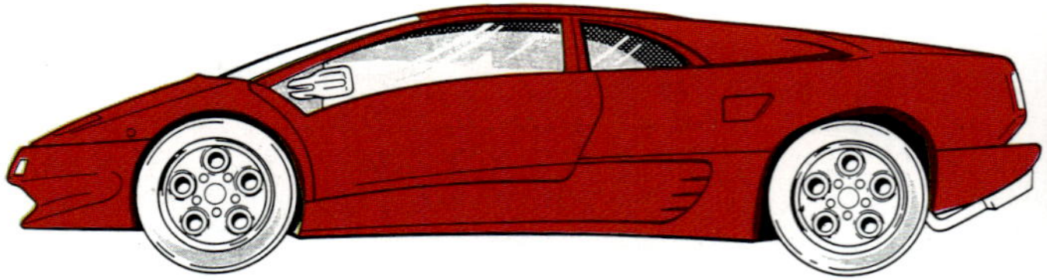

224.163 Diablo rosso met.

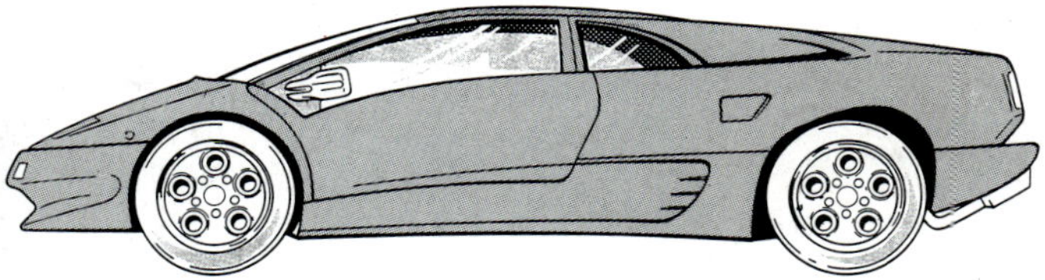

224.422 Silver mist met.

231.524 Deep black

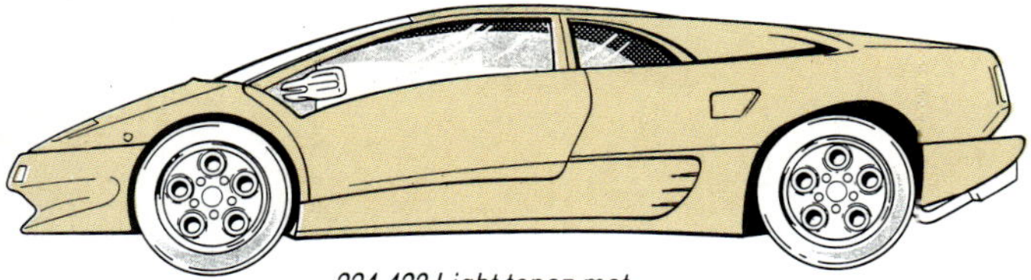

224.423 Light topaz met.

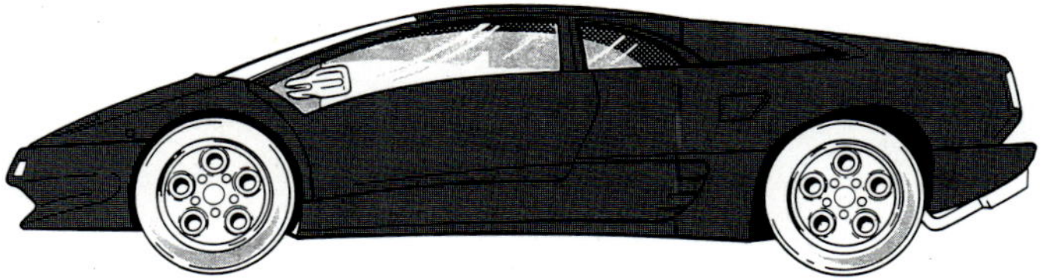

224.421 Agate grey met.

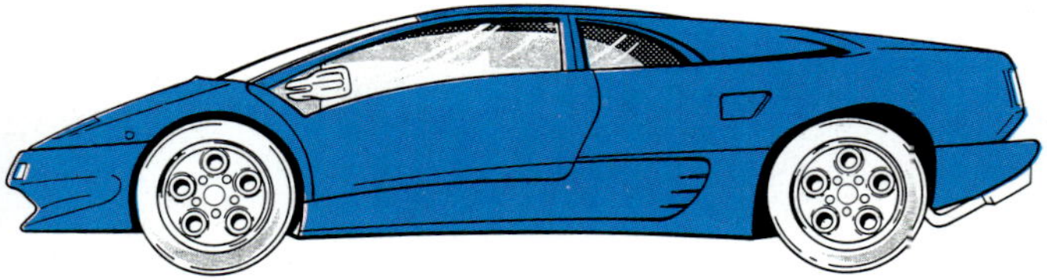

224.909 Bonzai blue met.

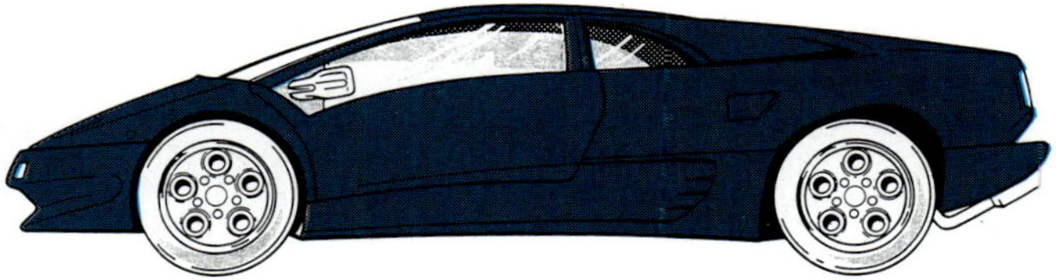

224.910 Midnight blue met.

Diablo

Opposite page. The front light clusters with retractable headlights, open and closed. This page, the light alloy OZ wheels, the side mirror and a close-up of the rear light clusters.

The doors open like scissors, like the Countach. Lamborghini advise not to weigh them down with things such as anti-theft devices, sound boxes and suchlike in order not to damage the sophisticated opening.

The doors which look like arms raised to the skies are a kind of gadget which delight the lucky owners and onlookers.

In the following pages, the engine bay which houses the powerful 12-cylinder and the interior, ergonomically designed for sporty driving.

The opening angle is a little larger than on the Countach, making access to the two seats a little easier.

Diablo

Lamborghini
Lamborghini

Even before the doors are opened, just viewed from outside, the Diablo gives a complete idea of the beast it is. Perusing its technical profile, we discover that it is 5 centimeters wider than the Countach, but this is not noticeable, because its lines are so soft and flowing. Nor does this flow diminish the aggressive power of this automobile, the intense, muscular energy that permeates from every piece of its bodywork.

Naturally the Diablo is not the Countach. The search for aerodynamic efficiency, with the rounding of all corners, definitely resulted in lines that are less aggressive than the absolutely astronautical forms of its illustrious progenitrix. But this is the inevitable consequence of the quest for efficiency. The Diablo was conceived from the start to reach a top speed of over 320 kph, so it is not enough to have a lot of horsepower: it also has to be light in weight and low in drag coefficient. The Countach, handsome though it was, had a high Cx, an almost indecent 0.40, while the Diablo boasts 0.31, with all the evident advantages in performance that implies. It is thus a handsome car that is efficient enough to justify a minimal sacrifice in visual impact.

The doorlocks, operated by an unusual-looking key, are opened by a button reset into the upper door moulding. The reciprocal positions of handle and button means the lefthand door can be opened conveniently with just the left hand and the same for the right side. Of course the doors, as on the Countach, open upward and forward. The opening angle is slightly larger, but the fact of having larger doors and lower doorsills makes the Diablo much easier to enter. The seats have been placed a little closer together and more centered, to reduce the pedal offset (now almost eliminated, though the footwell is still small) and gain some precious millimetres in headroom for the occupants. The driver's seat permits (and requires) several adjustments. No problem for the seats nor for the steering wheel, but the

There are very few cars which can top 300 kph. The Diablo is one of these but it also holds another record: it has the fastest unblown engine in the world.

problems begin with the two-level dashboard, which may undoubtedly be a good idea (particularly the nearness of the tachometer to the driving line of sight), but it must be adjusted minutely by a factory mechanic for each driver, if the driver wishes to see all the instruments easily. Part of this difficulty derives from the fact that a good idea like this one must have been ill-accepted by the person signing off on the final interior design, who did not devote much effort to finding the right position for each dial. In the more usual terrain of the central console, which actually contains only the climate- control selector, the clock and the stereo, and thus required no genial solutions, the problem was resolved in a tidy, efficient manner. On the whole, the interior of the Diablo is the part most susceptible to criticism, as it only partially digests the classic Italian GT style: the strip effect of the leather on the door panels resembles what we find on the average American sedan, the shape of the hand grip in front of the passenger is commonplace, there is no glove compartment worthy of the name (the one behind the seats is a laugh and, what's worse, when it is opened and closed, the seatbelts inevitably get caught in the lid). A word about the Breguet clock, whose characteristic hands on the *guilloché* dial would be as perfect for a fine, rather nostalgic wristwatch (but then the elegant anachronism of the wind reserve hand would be mandatory) as they are out of place in the linear futurism of the Diablo. Not recommended.

The steering wheel, pedals and shift lever are well arranged, however, better than in the Countach. The driving position is thus more modern and efficient, and the additional headroom is another plus. The controls for the lights, turn signals and various secondary functions are easy to reach and much improved with respect to the past. Once we are reasonably familiar with the commands, the moment has come to start the engine, always an important ceremony. The big 5.7-litre engine starts with a polite rumble that immediately subsides, leaving a purring idle (not exactly low: the factory recommends around 1250 rpm), with the accompaniment of a light hissing from the injection system. The power of progress.

There is no doubt that this Lamborghini injection is truly a fine complex. We must note that our nostalgia for the glorious old Weber 44 DCNFs fades into the background once we begin to appreciate the sweet running of this engine equipped with Lamborghini electronic injection (L.I.E.). The big 12-cylinder hums impeccably, without skipping a beat, promptly reacting, even cold, to the slightest caress of the accelerator (which, to act as a foil, has a rather strong return spring). In the takeoff phase, we note that the clutch has a

The flashing yellow Diablo sets off for the motorway. The Countach's complex but fascinating ignition procedure has been eliminated for the Diablo, thanks to the installation of electronic ignition.

A sophisticated engine such as the Diablo's calls for great precautions. Running in, for example is no less than 7000 km. In the first 2000 km it is absolutely forbidden to go faster than 190 kph.

stiff pedal like the brakes, the steering is naturally heavy at low speed, but that the visibility in all directions has been much improved over the Countach, making the Diablo much easier to get used to, despite its greater overall width. It is not exactly a subcompact in city traffic, of course, but it certainly isn't as difficult to approach as the Countach, which makes all neophytes sweat in the beginning. The gearshift is still rather stiff, especially cold. As we pick up speed it loosens up a bit but not excessively. The shifter is short, and is closer to the driver than the Countach's, in response to a widespread complaint about the distance of the latter. But this is not totally advantageous: the combination of a tall tunnel and a short shifter close to the seat leaves the right elbow rather too high for comfortable shifting, especially when whipping rapidly into third or fifth. One beloved detail of the Italian GT tradition has disappeared: the small metal tab with spring lock located on the shift gate at the entrance to reverse gear, to prevent accidental shifts.

As we begin to roll down the state highways, the Diablo's character becomes more clearly defined. The qualities of the new Lamborghini improve as it lengthens its stride. The powerful sound of the 12-cylinder is always pleasantly present. The suspensions are stiff but properly so, giving an exhilarating ultrasporty feeling, and at the same time they react more than adequately to the bumps and potholes of the Emilian roads, damping their effect without ever bottoming out or allowing the underpinnings to touch. The huge Pirelli P-Zeros play a role in this, and if the Diablo is the offspring of the Countach, they must accept the difficult hereditary role of the legendary P7s (still in production, of course). They perform their task impeccably, complementing the excellence of the suspensions without adding much roll noise, even though their "sound" changes perceptibly whenever the road surfacing changes. The fact that they kept Italian tyres on the image-making flagship is important, especially knowing that illustrious manufacturers like Bridgestone and Goodyear were contacted to produce tyres for the Diablo and participated enthusiastically in the competition for the supply contract. This means that the strong Japanese competition, and the less strong but still respectable American firm, must still bow to Italian capacity when it comes to this type of high-performance automobile, and we are quite happy about this. The chassis rigidity is exceptional: though we are mistreating the Diablo at high speed over the rough roadways, we note not the slightest flexing in any direction, which allows the suspensions to do their job correctly and thus get the maximum out of their excellent design. We feel it is

no dishonour to admit that the Diablo is one of those cars endowed with performance limitations, particularly regarding roadholding on dry surfaces, that significantly transcend the abilities of the less-than-professional driver. Except for expert race drivers, very few will be able to explore the full capabilities of this extraordinary automobile. Except on a modern racetrack, with its ample escape areas, the idea of taking a Diablo beyond its traction limits is as sensible as beating up on a pair of armed commandos in the center of Beirut, and the results comparable in terms of physical damage.

Then picking up speed, with the caution such a beast requires, we realize that it is so improved over its forerunner that any direct comparison would be a slight, and speaking of a "Countach 2" (as someone superficially suggested) is out of the question. The Countach's considerable understeer on most corners, for example, has been sharply diminished. The braking is powerful and safe, with good progressive modulation in the pedal effort. In other words, the "cold" mechanicals also offer the most one could desire at these maximum levels. And this, along with the significant progress in offering the Diablo driver a roomy, airy cockpit with ample window area, offers a great advantage in terms of the overall enjoyment of the latest supercar from Sant'Agata, not only compared to the Countach but also compared to its most direct competitor (which, we must repeat, is not the soft Testarossa but the much rougher F40).

Above everything stands the engine, however. In true Lamborghini tradition, this 12-cylinder offers the competition a benchmark difficult to equal and perhaps impossible to surpass. The lightning acceleration of this car, which reaches 100 kph in 4.09 seconds from a standing start, is only a hint of how powerful the engine is, with characteristics such as maximum power of 492 HP (362 kW) at 7,000 rpm and torque of 580 Nm (!) at 5,200 rpm, in the catalyzer version with 95 RON fuel. Even more immediately astonishing, especially for the layman, is the sensational top speed of 325 kph, for which part of the credit goes to the fine body design and its incredibly low drag coefficient (Cx of only 0.30). No, the most impressive thing is how flexible and pleasurable this 500-HP monster is to drive, and this can also be appreciated on the freeway, where you must take the Diablo to see what stuff this new bull-bearing monster is made of. Not until you have three rather uncluttered lanes to play with, in fact, can you truly press down with your right foot, clearing the throat of the powerful 12-cylinder, unleashing its 500 horses at least in the bottom three gears without worrying about the narrow road, the patrolman behind the billboard and so forth.

A welcome rest for the Diablo. The firm advises not turning the engine off after a sustained period of hard driving, but to let it turn over in neutral for a minute.

Driving the Diablo at the limit of its performance requires above normal driving ability. At the same time it is a car which in normal conditions of use has great drivability.

The roar that escapes the rear power plant instantly dispels any doubts that the fuel-injection system may have "effeminated" the Lamborghini engine. Despite the noise-abatement devices, catalytic converters and other such niceties, the Diablo displays a sound character equal to its road behavior, which we would be tempted to describe as doughty, harsh and fiery, if the Bard had not already used this terminology (we wonder what car the Merchant of Venice was trying out...). The acceleration is impressive: this is undoubtedly the fastest road car we have ever driven, and at the same time its progression doesn't stop at 100 or 200 kph. What's more, this doesn't require constant use of the gearshift. We tool along at 100 kph in fifth with light pressure on the accelerator and a distinct rumble of the engine at just 2,000 rpm. We need only tromp down on the gas pedal, however, and the music changes instantly. It is not necessary to shift down: just hold the foot down and the car picks up speed with the rapid, impartial progression of a good turbine. At 200 kph, the Diablo turns at only 4,000 rpm, and this is where its real territory begins. If the engine had good pickup between 2,000 and 4,000, it behaves even better above this level, thrusting the Diablo's nose into the atmosphere with a disconcerting quickness, and this at over 5,000 rpm (i.e. 250 kph). It continues to accelerate even though the counterpressure of the air becomes proportionally stronger, but here the Diablo truly flexes its muscles, and if you have the foot and the courage (as well as a few kilometres of traffic-free *autobahn*) you can experiment with relative safety and without excessive drama the emotion of driving the speedometer needle over the 300 mark. To go beyond this, it would be a good idea to be on the oval track at Nardò or something similar (where the series Diablo touched a real 327 kph). But what is most striking is the lack of troubles up to the magic figure of 300. Sure, it takes effort and concentration, but also an engine screaming like a banshee, nose glued to the road, perfect traction, the feeling of "having control" of the car, in other words, even at these lofty levels of performance. A truly exceptional result that crowns the Italian firm's efforts with success.

After our brief flight on the freeway, the return to the base allows us to savour other pleasant details, worthy corollaries of the Diablo's excellent mechanical qualities. The heat produced under maximum engine effort in the Diablo can be described as infernal (no pun intended), but it is dissipated in a highly efficient fashion by the cooling system. Perhaps this will mean less enjoyment for those languishing behind you in the summertime toll-booth queues, washed by the mass of hot air pushed out

The desire at least to come near the Diablo's limits cannot be held back. The Lamborghini designers have had therefore to concentrate much of their efforts on building a car with high active and passive safety.

by the rear fans. The climate- control system also works well and keeps the cockpit cool when the engine is under maximum stress or idling in a queue in the sun. The seats are perfect, highly sporty but comfortable and extremely well- profiled. The luggage compartment is not a fake rear cargo space (that covers the voluminous exhaust system) but is in front, and though of modest dimensions it is still sufficient for the soft leather carry-alls you need for a fast weekend at Monte Carlo with Cindy Crawford, but not for a soirée wardrobe.

The Diablo thus possesses a series of road qualities so convincing that it leaves no room for criticism. The engine is as powerful as a true Lamborghini needs to be, i.e. even too much so. The suspensions and tyres, as we said, work fantastically well together (and also offer a reasonable level of comfort). The brakes are simply exceptional and stop the car, which is no lightweight, in truly short distances without the minimum hint of fatigue. On the road, this car proves to be the mechanical jewel we all expected, and hats off to Marmiroli and friends for succeeding in this difficult undertaking. For one thing, the Diablo, precisely because of its evolution even in mentality with respect to the Countach, is unconceivably easier and more friendly to drive, and this is a pleasure. This is a robust, sincere cordiality that offers a lot only if you are willing to make a reasonable effort, not least of all the healthy muscular effort required by all the controls and a good dose of concentration in every maneuvre, even in simply keeping the car straight on those famous beat-up state roads mentioned earlier. In other words, it is a truly extraordinary *Grande Routière* for the "Real Men" of the 'nineties, a car with the beauty and capacity to makes us sad to contemplate the host of limitations high-speed traffic is heir to, even when it involves vehicles beyond discussion like this one. A car like the Diablo should be sold with an implicit (or even explicit, if possible) authorization to overlook the speed limits imposed on mass motoring. And its drivers, apart from the many hundreds of thousands of dollars needed to procure the keys to the car, should have to give assurances they will always operate this extraordinary car correctly at the maximum level. Utopia? Sure. But, after all, such an extraordinary car deserves it.

The Diablo is a supercar, but unlike the Ferrari F40, its boot will hold two suitcases and a couple of bags.

*Automobilia wishes to thank
Lamborghini Automobili SpA
for material and for their valuable contribution.*